T0169942

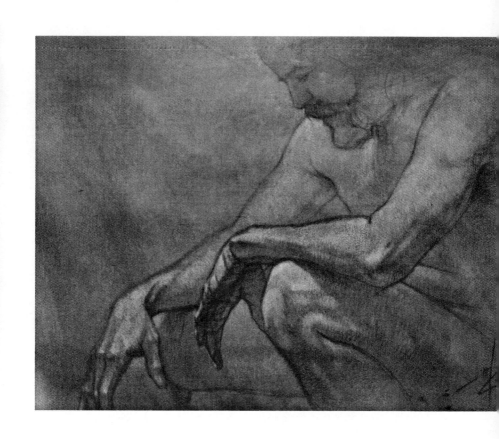

*Sometimes*

# Ashes of Light

*poems by*

## Lyubomir Levchev

*translated by*
Valentin Krustev
with additional translations
by Jack Harte

*artwork by*
Mark Gerard McKee

CURBSTONE PRESS

A Lannan Translation Selection
with Special Thanks to Patrick Lannan and
the Lannan Foundation Board of Directors

FIRST EDITION, 2006
Translation copyright © 2006 Valentin Krustev and Jack Harte
Artwork copyright © 2006 Mark Gerard McKee
All rights reserved.

Printed on acid-free paper by BookMobile
Cover art and design: Mark Gerard McKee

This book was published with the support of
The Griffis Foundation and the Lannan Foundation, with
supplemental support from the Connecticut Commission
on Culture and Tourism, and donations from individuals.
We are very grateful for this support.

Library of Congress Cataloging-in-Publication Data

Levchev, Liubomir.
  [Poems. English. Selections]
  Ashes of light / by Lyubomir Levchev ; translated by Valentin
Krustev ; with additional translations by Jack Harte ; artwork by
Mark McKee.— 1st ed.
    p. cm.
  ISBN-13: 978-1-931896-30-6 (pbk. : alk. paper)
  ISBN-10: 1-931896-30-5 (pbk. : alk. paper)
  1. Levchev, Liubomir—Translations into English. I. Krustev,
Valentin, 1949- II. Harte, Jack. III. Title.
  PG1038.22.E9A2 2006
  891.8'113—dc22                      2006004242

published by
  CURBSTONE PRESS   321 Jackson Street   Willimantic, CT 06226
          phone: 860-423-5110   e-mail: info@curbstone.org
                  http://www.curbstone.org

# Acknowledgments

The author wishes to thank the following magazines in which some of these poems first appeared: *The Café Review, Common Ground Review,* and *roger.*

Special thanks also to the Lannan Foundation for its ongoing commitment to the art of translation and to The Griffis Foundation and The Griffis Arts Center for remarkable support of artistic exchange between Bulgaria and the United States.

Thanks, also, to Jane Blanshard for proofing and copy-editing the manuscript, to Migdalia Salas for her fine support of my poetry in the US, to Curbstone's Judith Doyle for her careful attention to design, and to Alexander Taylor for traveling to Sofia to consult with the author and translator and for his many helpful suggestions for these English versions.

# CONTENTS

*Ashes of Light*

*Steps*

# GIMMEBREADYE

My friend,
what makes you sad?...
You look so wretched today.
Take a cigarette.
Let's have a smoke...

The smoke is growing like a tree
bearing dreams.
And its fruit is ripe,
and sweet,
and bitter.

Listen, if you want I can tell you
about Gimmebreadye...
...The snow is falling,
falling,
as if it wants to cover up the dark.
While the dark keeps gushing from beneath the drifts...
And wind,
wind whistles...

The homeless urchin's
little feet come to a halt
in front of our door.
And through the iron keyhole,
a frozen voice implores:
"Gimmebreadye!..."

It is my barefoot contemporary.
He carries wood and coal
to earn some bread.
That's why they call him Gimmebreadye...

And off he sets, carrying the huge buckets.
I follow him—
with the key to open the basement—
and then Mom stops me at the door:
"Watch out he doesn't swipe something down there!..."

Going down the staircase I wonder:
what could he swipe?
Both his hands are busy
with the buckets, right?...

Yet the great thief
swiped my heart!...

A pure smile:
"Do you know how to smoke?"
And we are buddies now
smoking from the same cigarette.
And I am choking from the smoke
and listening,
listening...
as if I were the single soldier
of that fairy country
where he's the great king,
his throne the upturned bucket.

I watch that daring profile
and listen to his wondrous words:
how one day
he'll hit the road
and catch up with the circus.
And then become a famous clown
with a humped back
and a cardboard nose
in the bright arena...
And he will let me in for free...

Gimmebreadye—the poorest of all on earth—
is sitting on his throne.
And everyone's so small before his laughter...
And the entire earth
is but a grain
of wheat.

...My friend,
when I feel wretched
and failures whip my heart,
and earthly days start tasting bitter,
and I feel like crying,
an enormous clown stands up
with a humped back and a cardboard nose...
And laughs,
and laughs, that clown,
when I am crying!...

1957

# CONTINUOUS POEM

Many nights
before the nativity
of our great intimacy
we would meet
like glances.

"And what are you thinking of now?"

We would meet
like lips:

"And what are you thinking of now?"

Suddenly
one evening
we began
to read each other's thoughts.
We smiled simultaneously.
Quite simply—we set forth.
With an embrace
I was shielding you from the wicked rain.
And the shopwindows were gilding us.
The sidewalks reflecting us.
The drivers scolding us.
Matrons laughing at us.
And all our former lovers
were playing for us
on distant trumpets...

We were flying
and we asked the shadows,
the winds,
the stars,
the rainpipes

and the phone booths:
A spot for two lovers!—
in the Library Park.
A spot for two lovers!—
under the Maritza power plant's chimneystack.

A spot for two lovers!—
on the Bourgas seawall.
A spot for two lovers!—
how small our Earth is!

A spot for two lovers!—
How short our days are!

How long will we have to fly
looking for a spot
for two lovers?

1962

# THE LAND OF THE MURDERED POETS

Between the Arctic Circle
and the Tropic of Cancer
(between passion
and thought)
and so far from heaven!—
there blooms a land,
beautiful
and abundant—
the land of the murdered poets...

Yet verses come forth.
They well up dark.
They tear me to pieces.
And behold,
like a tradition,
the woman reaper makes a swipe
to reap
a wisp of sunny rays.
"But you're alive!"—
The eagle takes offense.
The wolf's eyes search for my wounds.

A land for me!
A land deep within me!
You call from hours bereft of sleep.
And the mad Maritza river of my blood
is eating away the banks
of my heart.
And I am learning
to write down verses
in the land of the murdered poets.

1962

# WE STOPPED

We stopped.
Right under
the sign
"No stopping!"
and then you said to me:
"This is my favorite spot..."

A bridge
of rails and planks.
Oh, rusty rainbow!
And a sign:
"No stopping!"

Yet, no river flows beneath the bridge.
Railroads flow there.
And semaphores
wave their wings.
And roar the midnight shuntings.

And when
the locomotives rattled
under our feet,
clouds of steam enveloped us.
And totally invisible,
and totally alone,
we kissed each other.

Perhaps there are millions of cars
loaded with our kisses
sent out far and wide
across the world.
We were about to leave,
when I said to you:
"This is my favorite spot..."

A bridge.
Magical.
And unforgettable.

Between childhood and adulthood.
And a sign:
"No stopping!"

1962

*Stopping prohibited*

# MORNING

Yes,
the dark wind is full of the clanging of alarm clocks.
Hurry up, my boy!
Yes,
the milkmaid is delivering the morning
in jars and in plastic cups.
Hurry up!
They'll turn us away!
Yes,
our mouths are breathing clouds.
Yes,
we look like dragons.
One of us—big,
and the other one—smaller
and not yet quite awake...
Hurry up!
At the kindergarten door
the little dragon lets go of my hand:
"And can you for once come
and pick me up first,
while all the dolls are crying 'mama'
and all the hobbyhorses gallop
but aren't heading home.
Can you?"
"I'll try, my dragon child..."

I can summon the past.
I can penetrate the future.
I can crush with verse
my most malicious foes.
And I tell death that I'm a man...
Yet could I for once...

Yes,
The dark wind is full of the clang of alarm clocks.
And the dark wind is me.
And fathers are awakening in me.
How odd,
one of my hands is warm
the other—cold.

1964

# AND HERE I AM

To Bistra

And look: here I am waiting again
for the big love to come.
And look: here I am looking again
at the big clock.
On the big hand
a dove has perched
alone
like me.
Red clouds fume
in the afternoon silence.
And look:
the big clock hand
ticks;
it drops down a notch.
The dove's wings explode.
The frightened bird flies off
like an Egyptian soul.
I watch above the rooftops
a lost minute flitting
and disappearing.
And
the fear of the dove
sticks in my heart.

1964

# DÉNOUEMENT

You are undressing as if for the doctor.

Such thought fractures in my mind.
And suddenly
everything turns fragile.
The little vase becomes a test tube,
and the flower—some strange bacillus.
And you laugh aloud at me:
"Come on, come on!
Ask me how I'm feeling.
And what my trouble is.
And where it hurts...
Ask whatever you want!
Just don't pretend.

And I bend down mechanically.
"Take a deep breath!"—
          I say.

And the air takes you deeply in.
And you disappear.
You're no longer here.
The bed still clasps your warmth—
the torn clothes of a fugitive.
But you've broken loose.
Forever.

Most likely you are now
descending
down memory.
You're crying.
And the zipper of your skirt is torn.
And your voice is broken.

I hear:
Goodbye,
      darling,
            goodbye!
Goodbye, my craved-for one!
I wish you all the best—
and some of the pain.

1968

*Between Here and There*

# CAPRICE NO. 1

If I should have a career someday
(and they maintain it is inevitable),
if I should rise so high
that they start phoning me from everywhere,
then
I will appoint death as my secretary.

And when you phone and ask for me,
She'll say that I'm not in.
"But perhaps...
            just for a moment..."
"No!"
      she'll say,
                  "He is definitely not here!"
And all the while through that infinite time
I'll be gazing out the window
at how the leaves are falling,
or turning green,
at how the distant church dome resembles
a demitasse, turned upright for telling fortunes,
at how the girls look at themselves in glass doors,
and at how you are thinking that I am absolutely gone.

                                        1968

# CAPRICE NO. 2

Dammit!
This world is so mercurial,
    so entertaining
    and so kind
that it starts reminding me
of the house of a hanged man!
And I am giggling.
I am wandering the streets
with some friend of mine
who figures out the cunning game
to look at the women first in the face
and then guess what their legs are like.
And I am giggling.
We go on playing, each one on his own account.
And I am giggling...

Yet how I feel like talking about the rope!
Ah, how I feel like talking about the rope!...

1968

# CAPRICE NO. 3

I.
You.
The blank walls.
The night everywhere.
The windows filled with whiskey.
The girl's warmth.
You.
The wind.
The fantasy of the stars.
The falling of a leaf upon the asphalt.
The wind...

Oh, split second, stop!
        Look!
        Listen!
        And then go.
Unless Doctor Faustus is coming—
having found an excuse for everything.

1968

# POETRY READING

Poetry readings,
poetry readings!...
From the small students' clubs
     to the triumphal halls,
against windmills,
and against ghosts,
in dreadful working days
yet without chain armor...
The poet follows his poetry all life long,
as Sancho follows his Don Quixote!

Well, of course,
each has received his bouquet of flowers.

But there are those distant small towns!
A railway stop.
Dogs barking.
Mounds of beets and empty crates...
And look—
we
slowly
fall out of the evening train.

And beneath the little signal-bell waits for us
that ill-at-ease kid—
our eternal
     and unknown
          confrere,
who has called us like spirits into his world.

Always "on behalf of all the enthusiastic construction workers,"
who are said to be "lovers of poetry readings"...

All right!
We set off as silent as a patrol.
The shortcut resembles a field.

But ahead of us
          like heroin
                    excitedly shines
the electric flower of the construction site.
And in Canteen Number 2,
amid the smell of stew,
we are adressing
     you,
          twentieth century:

          "You are blood-stained
          with dreams
          and delusions!
          You need
                    crazy poets!..."

     "We will sweep your heavens free of mines!..."

Ah, we are promising raavishing miracles!
But the handful of fitters
                    who have come to hear us,
aren't enchanted—
they go out for a smoke.
Straight bewilderment shines blue in their eyes:
"What are these artists agitating us for?..."

Poets can survive everything—
being hungry,
and yet sing,
being unemployed,
expelled students...

But, my God,
                    can one possibly do without applause?
Grin a bit!
Say it doesn't matter.
But a hole will appear in your soul—
                              defeat!
                                   Defeat!


And so
how often
in dining cars
we would wash away our wounds with brandy.
And someone would sigh
with tragic irony:
"And Zhenya Evtushenko gives readings in stadiums!
That's how it is,
                    with Russians
                         my friend—
they listen to you, even if you're not that great...
And even when they don't understand a thing,
still in some place like New York,
                    they will applauad you..."


"Oh, no!
Stadiums are not for poems!
Poems are read in sacred hours.
Like love letters.
Like secret leaflets
which require not demonstrations,
                    but dedication!..."


But
the return train would stop
          and the poets would disperse
to their old lodging places,
          to their new battlefields...

21

Along the park,
along the stadium,
I, too, happened to be returning late...

when all of a sudden I spotted
that the fence was ripped down.
And a smile dawned on me.
And like a thought from the past I passed through it
and past the deserted bleachers
                    to the immense crater.
A discarded bottle
clattered down the steps,
like an absurd bell
in the absurd amphitheater.

And then...
Then I was overtaken
          by that romantic adventure.
Three billion stars
were sitting on the bleachers, all staring at me.
And I began to recite
in a surprising voice.
And my sincerest passions
echoed selflessly in the dark.
I think I was telling the stars
how man rises.
And how difficult it is for him to shine all life long.
Yet with his own light,
reduces himself to ashes
over new foundations
                    or over honest stanzas...

If there had been a watchman,
          he would have thought I had gone mad.

But you know
I couldn't care less
about that.
So real was this poetry reading of mine
that I permit you to envy me!

1968

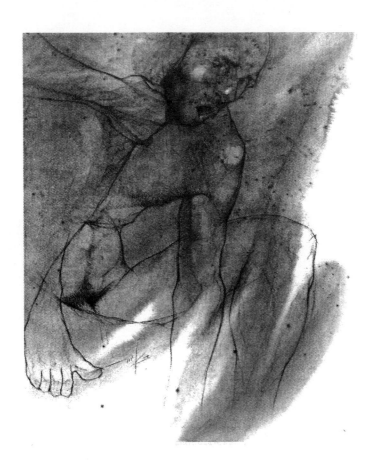

*Lazarus*

# ROOFS

*To Bogomil Rainov*

Old Grandpa's house
had a roof made of slate.
I remember, there were even some weeds
growing there...

"Where is,"
    I ask,
        "grandpa's old house?"
And they answer, it collapsed
on its own.
"Look,"
they say,
"we created an original sidewalk
with the roof-slate!"

...Of course, the slate is the same.
As for the house having collapsed
on its own...
        I absolutely can't believe it!

It was an oddly built house:
cozy,
simple,
human...
However, both grandpa's universe
and it
      had the same defect—
a goddamn heavy roof
and no foundations.

So, the house has not collapsed
but has slowly,

slowly sunk into the earth.
It has sunk right up to the roof.
And today I walk on its slate like a cat.
And box shrubs smoke through the chimneys...
While down below—
        in grandpa's Atlantis—
everything is as it was in the old days.

The hearth is burning.
Dried beans are simmering in the earthenware pot.
And daddy—
        a tiny little boy—
                        cuddles in grandma's lap.

"Go to sleep now!"
            she whispers,
"for the bogeyman is walking on the roof!..."
And daddy listens horror-stricken.
Yes, he can hear it!
(It's my steps.)
And he believes.
And shivers.
And falls asleep...

Meanwhile, I keep stamping on the sidewalk.

Constructing roofs, so the base of time
can bear them, is fiercely difficult.

The superstructure
        (Marx would say)
should not crush the base!
And we—the writing ones—
must figure out something very true,
realistic,

sunny
and sturdy...

Because, I think,
       somebody
is already walking on the roof.
And lightning-flashes,
like wings,
are sprouting from his shoulderblades.

1971

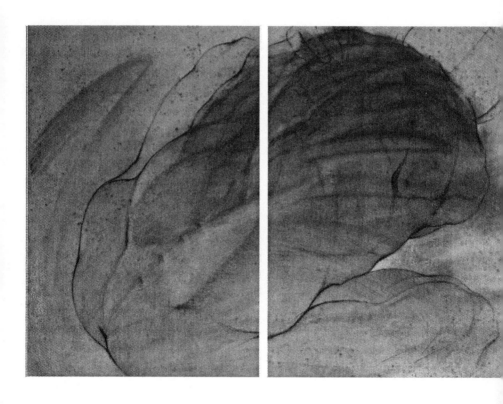

*Morangosov*

# CAPRICE NO. 4

Happiness,
they say,
is the slaughterhouse of poets.
But it's not I who said it.
Happiness,
they say,
real happiness,
is as scattered throughout our lives
as life perhaps is scattered
throughout the universe.
    Light-year distances!
    Light-year desperations!
But don't be afraid, my friend,
of being all alone
in space,
of being all alone
in time,
of being all alone
within yourself...
Like Prometheus and the rock.
Like Joan of Arc and the bonfire.
Like Levski and the hangman's rope.
Like happiness
and the poet.

1974

29

# CAPRICE NO. 6

It's true that I am overburdened.
It's true that I carry a cargo of memories.
It's true that some are forbidden and dangerous...

I'm sailing with a list like some doomed ship.
"We'll sink!"—
the captain shouts from within.
"It's possible"—
I say—
        " but I won't jettison anything."

"The first big wave will send us down
to dine with the girls from Atlantis!"
"Well, okay, okay..."
I'll try not to worry too much...

And isn't it obvious that I am calm?

I cross the "Sound of Sweet Fatigue."
I heave to in the "Bay of Whispers."
Your hand is burning in my hand
like a covered lantern.

The park swings are rocking on their own,
like in the old days
when I was invisible.

And only their metallic exclamation is heard,
or the grating of armor
from some saga
or from some somber ballad...

There my youth is calling:
Love,
how much you have given me!
Love,
how much you have taken from me!

But today I don't need your words!
I only need your voice.
I throw myself into it.
I hide my head as in my mother's lap.
I wriggle happily.
I'm sinking,
ever deeper,
ever deeper.
To where
girls from Atlantis
bring me amphoras of fragrant madness.

1976

# CAPRICE NO. 7

I drank of insincere feelings.
I drank because I was dying of thirst,
     because I was parched,
     because I was already cracking.
I drank of insincere feelings—
deceptive,
sticky,
sweet swift-flowing transience!

I drank...
and now I feel sick.
In the West the sunset is painting
a portrait of my absence.
The bells are tolling.
God is drinking, too.
And in my eyes snow-covered wastes extend...

Oh how I hope my face won't betray me!
I offer my entire kingdom
for just one smile!
Why didn't I die of thirst!

1978

# CAPRICE NO. 11

The Sacred Volcano—
that woodcut,
carved with a few scratches
by Hokusai,
shines in my mind
more powerful than reality
and far more true than nature.

For the real mountain,
the real Fujiyama—
it's
so improbable
I could accept it only
as a dream,
as a sigh,
as an interjection.
Ah...

Its foot is lost
in a mist of tenderness.
Only its snow-capped crown
gleams in the sky like a phantom,
like a balcony,
but
one that projects from the void of the universe
from the castle of the unknown.

I wouldn't believe my eyes
if I didn't know
that such a celestial
balcony
floats incredible
in me.

Once in a few million
years
you step out on it,
my love.
You step out to see if there are any stars.
But instead you discover
the murderous
dark
man.

I love you!
This whisper at the very end,
this final word,
having thrown out all its meaning
so it can carry
all its feeling.
I love you!

No.
That's no word.
That surely is the ultimate particle
that's left of me.
The ultimate real something
that I have.
Take it!

1980

# THE GARDEN BEFORE PARADISE

The Field Marshal went by.
He didn't like the town.
The tanks went by.
The trucks went by.
And only a bumpy road remained.
And a hundred injured horses.

A sentimental commander
had made a strange gesture—
he had given a team of horses
freedom and peace...
And this during wartime hunger.

These weren't graceful circus performers
nor slender-legged steeplechase jumpers.
These were warhorses,
made deaf by guns,
blind by fire,
horses with spotless honor.

Decorated with monstrous wounds,
they grazed slowly in an orchard,
and drank long from the stone trough
their last sacrament
before going
to Paradise.

No one shod them anymore.
Only the nightingales sang their evening praises.
Only one very old soldier was detailed
to take care of them
and like them
finish his life.

His entire family had been killed long before.
All of them were buried in his absence.
And now
he buried the horses
like a centaur.
He would fire once in the air
and make the sign of the cross.

There he is—
in front of the straw hut,
well-groomed,
with all his medals and insignia,
having passed through all the bloody dramas
and having hidden all his pain beneath a simple pride.

We, the children, used to bring him cigarettes and matches,
which we'd swipe from our fathers and brothers.
But he would accept no presents,
so we'd leave them there beside him,
on the grass.

He recognized our passion for riding,
our passion for the frightful,
our passion for what was forbidden...
And with a simple nod of his head,
he would point at the horses
allotted to us.

The wounded horses would give us a gentle lick
while we climbed up
barefoot
by their manes.
And they would set forth heavily—
with a warlike gait,
they—for the last time—

we—for the first time—
happy.

We lived long, but we did not grow old
and they did not kill us.
And now when I hear
that Shiva
is dancing
again,
I hear my heart howl distantly and quietly.
"Captain,
it's useless to undergo any treatment!
Our flesh isn't even good for horse-sausages.
And if we survive this last battle till the end,
make your strange and dangerous gesture—
let us in to die
in the garden before Paradise."

1989

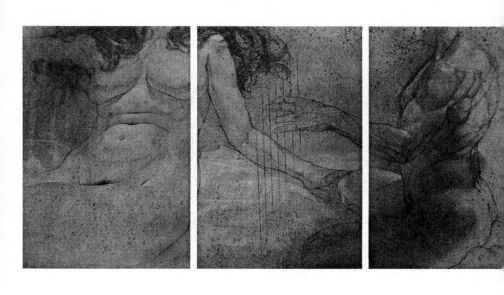

*Legend*

# LETTER
*Poste Restante*

The red luminary takes leave.
The last wild lynx peers into
what's invisible to us.
The snow on the summits takes leave.
The motionless lift-cabins
travel on towards oblivion,
travel on.
Like a dream driven away.
Like a desperate hope.
The epoch takes leave.
Ecstasy takes leave.
And it seems only I am left.

I don't know if I'll be able to write to you again.
I don't know if I'll be able to see you.
But I know there is no way I could forget you
until the end
and maybe even after that.

I'll leave my keys in the door of nonexistence.
I'll leave my glasses and go blind.
I'll be looking for you with bleeding fingers
but everything I touch
will burn to ashes.
I'll forget your name.
I'll forget to breathe.
And only your tenderness will flow instead of time.
And only your whisper in the ear of darkness...
OK!
I heard...
Goodbye!
Goodbye!

Goodbye!
Goodbye!

At which slave market did you buy me
and leave me, before you set me free?
What is it that I hold tight in my sunken heart?
Even if I knew
I would no longer tell you.

1989

# LOVE IN THE MILITARY HOSPITAL

Night's greatcoat is large for us—
It will cover us both and still trail on the ground.
It will cover our tracks and just
our words will remain

to wander about and find each other sometimes.

It so happens I've bid farewell to arms,
yet in such a way that God
will remember me.
But I have never been in any military hospital.

By the quiet poisonous Don
I have rolled
sabered by Cossack girls' eyelashes.
But I have never been in any military hospital.

Among stars and sand and plague
with the dreadful artist Gro
I have contemplated the visit of the great mirages.
But I have never...
Yet, yesterday
we were in the military infirmary.
Covered by the greatcoat—
like a puddle
among puddles of clotted and not-yet-shed blood.
Among piles of pus-stained bandages and gauze
and Heavy Metal chains
we lay embraced, no,
clung to one another.

You had stopped my fatal wound with a kiss
and my soul was flowing out

not into chaos and the pitch dark
but into you, my light abyss.

At the bottom. That's where I wished to hide myself.
We were trembling, both of us.
While around us were screaming the blind, the amputated,
the drugged, the doomed...
they were vomiting death screams:
"Allons enfants! Allons enfants!"
"Egalité!" "Fraternité!"
The sailor with the cut-off legs
broke into a song with his last inspiration:
"Rot Front!"—the armless raised his arms.
"Avanti populo!"
"¡No Pasarán!
"Za Stalina, za Rodinu!"
"Za Stalina!..."—
the punitive squad was shouting,
as well as those—the Other Ones,
the almost buried in the thirty-million-graves ones.
"¡Patria o muerte!"
"¡Venceremos!"

And maybe I am also blind already.
And that's why I am caressing you like mad.
I read you like Braille: "Forgive me!"
And you whisper: "Not that! Say that other thing!
Say it to me again!"
And I shout: "I love you!" like someone just convicted.
The way one cries out his last word.

Don't worry, they won't hear us
in the twentieth-century military infirmary
among all these screams, moans,
curses, wheezes,
and residual silence.

When tomorrow morning the gravediggers come for me,
speak up again and say you've already burned me.
Say that's what I wanted—to be burned separately.
Don't say that you mean your fire.
As for my name, it may stay with the Other Ones
in the common grave...
But even that's too much.
Better claim until the end
that I have never been in any military hospital.

1989

# I WHO DID NOT FLEE POMPEII

Death is a mystery. A fear... But hardly an end.
Earth's cradle rocks me in the void.
And I hear the spheres—the crystal-clear signals—
I who did not flee Pompeii.

Before the excavations brought me forth
curled like an embryo, silent, petrified—
I simply withstood the brunt of elements.
And the perishable clung to me.

I watched you running down the slope
toward boats and lifesaving lies.
Having robbed the temples, you prayed
your sin was blamed on someone else.

Men. Beasts... Everything vanished.
How beautiful Pompeii the waste was!
A few blades of grass stayed with me.
And glory crept up slowly like a villain.

God was replaced. They studied the Volcano.
The corrupt city has become a museum.
And only I remained here with myself,
I who did not flee Pompeii.

                                        1994

# SO MANY RELIGIONS

For Betty Chu

So many religions! Such splendid temples!
And not a single solace for the mind.
A cold expanse.
A lonely ocean wafting
greetings from Labrador.
Belfries—
golden steeples—
ampoules thrust into the sky,
needles
stuck into nonexistence...
And it no longer hurts.
And the sunset is a drug addict.
And no new romance begins.

1996

# THE SUNLIT SHIP

Then the sunlit ship eases off
ceremoniously upriver.
I was fame's welcomer and seer-off.
Now I'm alone with my freedom.

After sunset the sky glows a long time
but the streets are totally empty.
Peacefully I become part of the silhouette
of the weary worldwide insanity.

Now someone else is playing with the stars.
Something twinkles there and advances.
Like a bee, having fled paradise,
under the moon an airplane passes.

1996

# MOONLESS CALENDAR

*The moon is an angel with a bright light sent*
*to surprise me once before I die*
*with the real aspect of things.*
*It holds the light steady and makes no comment.*
                                    —William Meredith

I.

Neither wolf, nor brother.
Man to man is Bulgarian.
Chaos comes with brand-new scales. And thereafter:
nightless days
and dayless nights.
Times, about which they used to say
there aren't such times!
Times about which...
you'd better not talk!
Look, you admit them and even harbor them.
In your inner self you watch them secretly and stunned.
Such rubble of life has never come this way before.
Fugitives from closed circles. Rapacious saints.
They squeeze
a broken clock hand in their fists.
And down their necks
broken cords are bleeding.
There aren't such days in the familiar calendars.
Except,...probably in one—
let's call it moonless.

II.

I call
but I don't baptize.
A calendar. A series. A caravan of tired troubles.
Let it trail like that!

Let it seek its God...
With days like these, unable
to repent,
or to forgive.

III.

No
nonmigratory bird is seen.
Not a single
evergreen plant.
The foliage slides away under acid rain,
providing us the knowledge
that there isn't even a providence.

IV.

And when everything collapsed, and renounced itself, and fled,
in the solitude that reigned,
only a single child's dream remained by my side
and several madmen.

V.

Perhaps they were that Mouncho's sons?
No!
I could not remember who they were.
While they...
They said they could not forget me.
They would keep coming
and in the great decline of commonsense,
we would walk as if through a wild wood.

VI.

They were darkly wretched.
Moonlessly outcast.
With manners and clothes from another
unknown drama.
They had come to the wrong stage, mistaken the words and
                                                      the twilight.
But their feeling was right, they wanted to help me.
And in the hall of the Universe,
in the passersby age:
there was nothing to lean on but their crumpled shoulders.

VII.

In fact, I also felt like passing by. Fading completely.
In fact I had already recalled the Andes, and the huge birds.
The poet, who returned to his irretrievable Lima,
disgusted with laws, poisoned with pisco,
who had voluntarily entered an asylum for madmen and lunatics...
Maybe it's better to go your way in this mental derangement:
to think, speak and write whatever you please.

VIII.

My companions listened to me disapprovingly.
No! They didn't approve of the way poets think.
They had already tried the "voluntary" final asylum.
A romantic beginning.
But little by little you come to realize that the chief physician,
the master of the sick world, is the truly mad one.

IX.

It is not very pleasant
to make such a discovery
when he is holding your future
in his one hand
and in the other—the key to the secrets
that locks up so easily
and unlocks so hard.

X.

What was the need of all those disputes?
A well-known woman philosopher
was educating me in vain in "La Coupole":
"Art is a schizophrenia!
Power is a paranoia!"
Now, like that dead teacher, I want
to say or think:
"O lord, I am not worthy!"

XI.

This moonless sheet eclipses the heart.
The way the women eclipsed their windows
during the war.
You disappear from the outside
and remain inside yourself.
In this protected space your blinded stars
may come back holding one another.
And without being the ruler with Judaic name
a lightning may strike your heart.

XII.

Lightning flashes already. The air is sweet with ozone.
Liberty itself
chooses me among its instruments.
The theater of eternity is setting up its new
and totally unknown season.

1997

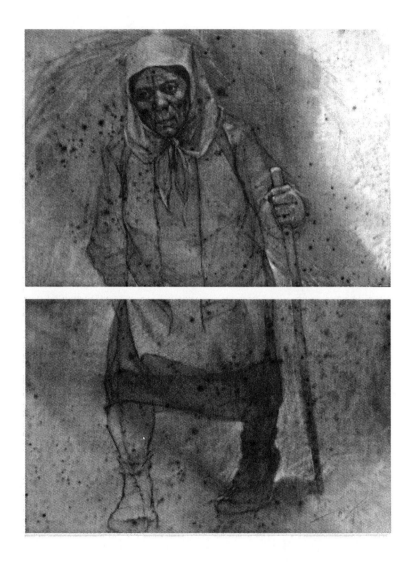

*Hay Carrier*

# TOMORROW'S BREAD

Once I reproached my son
because he did not know
where to buy bread.
And now...
he is selling bread
in America.
In Washington.
In his daytime routine
he teaches at the university.
At night he writes poetry.
But on Saturdays and Sundays
he sells bread
on the corner of Nebraska and Connecticut.

The fields of Bulgaria are empty.
Those women of the earth who used to
reap the crops to feed the generations,
are fading away like the notes of a dying song.
Politicians set up the melodrama:
"Who filched the wheat of the motherland?!"
But what lies between bread and man remains
hidden behind the several names,
different in taste and different in price.

My son sells bread for sandwiches,
rosemary buns, olive rolls,
"Zaatar" loaves, Spanish sesame "semolina",
walnut bread, wheat bread, sprinkled with raisins,
Italian "Pane Bello."
"Palladin," kneaded with olive oil, with yeast and milk,
corn bread, pumpkin-seed bread,
Turkish bread, bread made of clouds...
Only Bulgarian bread is not available,
nor the leftover bread from yesterday!

"Some bread remains unsold
every day," my son says.
"We are given a loaf for dinner.
The rest is wrapped in plastic bags
and dumped..."

Weariness weighs on my son.
The bread has handed him an American dream
(And this, too, means The American Dream)
Oh God, don't you hear? My son is praying for something!
Danger encircles him like an aura.

Give me the answer, Lord, to one single prayer—
to one last wish,
then do, please, whatever my son asks of you.
And sure, you might as well adopt him!

In Sofia
the shades of old women
scour the dark.
Ransacking the rubbish bins they collect bread.
Pointing at one of them, a teacher
of history and Bulgarian language, they say:

"Don't jump to conclusions, take it easy!
She's not taking the bread for herself. She feeds
stray dogs
and birds."

And my words too are food for dogs
and birds.

Oh God!
Why am I alive?
Why do I wander alone in the Rhodopes?

Why do I gaze down abandoned wells?
Why do I dig into caves where people lie?
And pass the night in sacred places, renounced by you?

I am seeking the way
to the last magician's hideout,
he who forgot to die
but has not forgotten the secret of bread.
Not today's bread, which is for sale,
not yesterday's bread which has been dumped...
I must know the secret of tomorrow's bread.
The bread we kiss in awe.
The bread that takes our children by the hand
and leads them all back home.

1998
*JH*

# LIGHTHOUSE

*To N. Bojilov*

Naked as an idol—
banned—
I am lying under palm-tree clouds,
buried alive in the finite sky...

But I'm preoccupied by other things.

Does one live on after it's over?
Or is there some other way of existence?
Or do only invisible traces of us
remain, which even the stellar Dogs
of the celestial Hunter lose?
Or is the astral space filled with souls,
the way my glass is filled with emptied glasses?

What does one do in Paradise?
I want to do something. The Paradise Rock
lies beyond the bend. But before that
I passed the white, solitary universe
where Jules Verne had been drawing up his prophecies.

On the other side of the gulf,
beyond the green mist,
Chagall
had been flying with or without violin...
Only those twisting stone-pines have remained from the song—
the game of azure features—
the game of *Nulla dies sine linea.*

But thought
scales other slopes.

Paths are quickly overgrown.
Wounds never close.
A different god has triumphed.
Let us hope he will be better.

I have never understood
who was the abandoned one—
me or the ocean.
There I buried the utopia and the compass.

Now I'm lying under the palm trees of Eden Rock.
Silver helicopters and hydroplanes
are humming and entering the flower of the sun.
They keep gathering wisdom,
until the evening settles in
and the discos on the beach
fill up with oblivion like honeycombs.

Then the lighthouse of Garoupe
like a cavalry horse
harnessed to a garden wheel
spins the world's wheel again.

The Moon, a silver ball,
bumps against the stars
and stops again on black!
And skepticism is in style again.

But my thought...

I have not staked it
on either a color or a number.

The human soul boils with love and peril.
The incest of constellations gives birth
to new illusions, new religions, and new apostles.
They are foretold.
They are called "second history."
It's them I count on.
And it's to them I send my signals.

But during the day the lighthouse of Garoupe
is only a pale ghost
southwest of old Antibes.

1998
JH

# PIER

*good, perhaps, for Noah*

On dry land
boats become other creatures.
They lie down,
deceiving,
persuading themselves
they've been hunted by the storm.
In fact, they are out of use.
To flow into moist sand—
now that's
the saddest self-foundering
for both boats and dreams!
The former already look like flowerpots.
Weeds make love inside them.
The latter are raised up like a fence,
a refuge against the wind.
And coals—black bones—
betray the secret of the fire,
where the oars have burned.
Close to the pier
a rotted boat
has hauled itself up on tiptoe, hull skyward.
A temple on piles. And within
sleeps a traveler or an ancient god.
He has abandoned his rigid mythology
and now sleeps on his stomach,
having turned his back on the skies...
His hand moves.
Perhaps
he has hunted the vexing full moon
or else he dreams he has flung
his harpoon towards some nebulous spirit.
Near the jetty, I am watching him, silently.

I'm scared that if I wake him
he will cry out, having rubbed his eyes:
"There's my image, disfigured
by its education, by morals,
by its nurture,
and by its frequent reformation.
He will die of jealousy
seeing me freer than he is."
"Not more free, but abandoned,"
I would cry out deliberately, no doubt.
He will continue to cry:

"Look at my original image.
He knows
neither his beginning nor his end.
He doesn't even know...
that in this world
imitation
precedes the image!"

1999
*JH*

# CAPRICE NO. 16

To Maria Stolarova

Something lies hidden in this not-entirely-discovered world.

Someone's breath penetrates
my spirit and lurks
behind the curtain of autumn.
Perhaps a fugitive dream waits
for reality to fall asleep. Or perhaps
the condemned sunset had breathed
its last sigh:
"Mother, the dark."

Hey, you, the Invisible One,
if you're a thief
take whatever you want:
Dreams. Illusions. Utopias.
These exquisite fantasies
won't make you rich
in this world of toughs and gangsters.

If you're a killer
you're too late!
The angelic-faced
moral maximalists are already ahead of you.
But what would it cost you
to try again?
Have another go, my friend!
*Repetitio mater studiorum est.*

If you're homeless—
stay!
The bread and wine are on the table.
Lie and tell them you're a friend

from the barracks. Or else,
that you are my time.
And you've already come.

But if you are the Messenger—
I am waiting for you.
If you wish to know the secret—
whether silence is deaf-mute,
or pretends to be a dead
thunder,
you should first recognize me.

In the mazes of the secret monster
or in Madame Tussaud's museum,
one hundred sorcerers created
one hundred poisonous doubles of me.
"They look real."
They represent
my hundred imagined suicides.

You'll find it difficult, Messenger,
but I know you'll recognize me.
You'll recognize me
by the aura of violet fatigue.
Then we'll sit down at the café
under the umbrellas on the sidewalk.
Then we will free ourselves of the secrets.
A lot of people will go by
disgusted with history.
They will look at me
with sympathy
and whisper to themselves:
Look at that one—
talking with himself without a cellphone.
Then I'll lean on the edge

where everything else begins.
And I'll only feel how love and freedom
merge within me.

1999

*Thirty Bird Boy*

# THE UNIVERSE IS AN
# ANONYMOUS CREATOR

For Charles Chu

That Chinese painter we spoke of,
for no reason that we can comprehend,
has turned into a painting by a Chinese
painter.
Nothing else about him is known.

We have other names,
a PIN, an ID chip, etc.
Yet, our soul remains impenetrable.

While he—the nameless one—exhibits
only a soul, exposed and lucid.

We contemplate the painting...
While he
through the thin peepholes of heaven's doors
carefully and silently examines us.

The Chinese painter, viewed
close-up, is astonishingly modern.
He breaks the visible lines
replacing them with secret links.
He makes signs out of things, and meanings—out of us.

However, viewed from a distance,
the Chinese painter
helps my soul
rid itself of time...
And now it makes no difference any more
                what dynasty rules over me.

The Chinese painter has taught me
to set the main idea in the corner,
not in the middle of the work.
Because if we consider the eternal, endless whole,
the empty space is central there.
Nonetheless, the little man—i.e. we,
standing down against the waterfall,
deaden it with our muteness.
Don't sign your work!
says the little man.
It's no use.
The Universe is an anonymous creator.

1999

# THE BOTTLES

I wake,
unlock my eyes
and go out of myself.
The first thing I encounter
are the empty bottles.
Oh, hi there!
I knew some things
wouldn't abandon me
while I'm wandering about in pink nightmares.
One-eyed,
like little cyclops,
they guard their caves.
And I remember Vanga,
that blind clairvoyant,
who said to Raphael Alberti:
"Poor Spaniard,
all your kin are already dead.
Here they are—
their souls come
and line up like bottles."
Since then I've been taking great care
of the bottles. Because
judging by their circle,
my family of drunks
was quite large.
They claim that the conversation
between the living and the dead
is never listened to.
But, just in case,
I'd better not rattle on
with these empty bottles.
It would be far better to put
an ad in the paper
for all those shipwrecked at the moment:

"Bottles offered—
including the letters
SOS! SOS!—
practically free!"
However,
in this world in which we are awake,
the shipwrecked are far more numerous
than all the ships.
And now no one
throws even a stony glance
at the chasm of the wreckage of others.
Whereas earlier,
with the dignity of the poor,
our mothers exchanged empty bottles
for bread.
Now even this is getting hard,
it seems.
Today, as far as I can see,
even the epoch
is searching for a depot
to deposit our empty words.
And likewise love
returns our empty illusions.
You too, empty heart,
go out and look for
a God who stays open 24/7
so that He might exchange your empty spaces
for a new bottle of the vintage
*Universe*—made in Bulgaria.

2001

# THE LAST CAPRICE

*In balance with this life, this death*
—W. B. Yeats

I am walking.
And I am leading my father by the hand.
And he is ever smaller and smaller.
He has lost the key to home.
But he will never admit it.
Like son, like father.
And actually now I don't know
where I could take him.
The Internet Café
is closed for prophylaxis.
Besides, I don't know
how to open the site
to the Hereafter.
I only know
that the world is a sentence
from a long apocrypha for gods.
And I am trying
to build up a home of words.
But it collapses on me.
And I shout
Oxygen,
help me burn down more quickly!
I feel intolerably wretched!
Iron,
I renounce you!
Damn you,
rigidness.
The world is a manner of expression.
Daddy,
I don't want to be a father!
I feel terribly wretched.

Mom,
I don't want to become older than you, either!
Allow me this last caprice.
Do something! Please!

You, who are already in the earth,
and the earth has always been in you,
say that you are the Goddess-Mother.
And that all things are my brothers.
Allow me to appeal to darkness.
And to sink forever
into her infinite embrace.

2001

# PATH

To Georgy Trifonov

Someone is pronouncing you, my friend.
Have you become a prayer by chance?
Someone is checking you like a pulse.
Yet the hand can scarcely feel you.

Stop talking nonsense! You'd better go out jogging.
And you set out. But you look around. And you finally see—
that someone has thrown a dead lamb
onto the path where you used to jog and dream.

The sky is clear. In fact, everything is clear.
The rabid fox barks from the bridge.
Then your soul is overgrown with quietude again.
But the gun's bead has already pinpointed you.

And don't say that these are country scenes.
The sign of the universe is the same everywhere.
Even this stinking twin brother of the Sphinx
reminds you of kings Oedipus and Lear.

The precipice moves its crumbling mouth,
prompting you: Jump down into me! Come on!
No. You will go on along the arrogant path.
No. The local one-hundred bagpipes aren't a whiskey brand!

Meanwhile death's skull snarls at the narrow pass.
The crow, the fox, and other characters
pick the carrion clean, change the epochs
and now you don't know whose carcass it is.

Maybe it's that of the little golden lion
that fell from your young hero's little fur cap
when you were in first grade,
leaving you secretly crying.

Today everyone's changing their color or course.
Like guitarists playing all positions.
Are you alone to remain on the merciless path—
strung like a bead on a rosary?

Stop counting prayers and curses.
Once the fox has bitten your footprint,
break the rosary, my friend, and let's disperse
into another, more real, freedom!

This idea, these wild oats
will barely strike a root in my nature.
I take the saddle off the epoch's back
and lie down in the grass to ride, half awake.

Then through dreamy eyelashes I see
how the true path flees from me, leaving me alone
It's so funny and I feel so carefree!
As if I have not yet been born.

2001

# THE GARDENS OF ETERNITY

Suddenly
the council of the winds is called.
The clouds remember they're relatives of yours.
And you hear:
"It's high time to take the child
to the zoo."

And you realize that this is a rebuke—a dangerous rebuke
about some quite other, forgotten promise.
And a dark-green morning lies in wait for you
beneath the torture-garden olive trees.

The seventh day has come again.
God is resting.
And you are created.
Entry to the zoo is free today.
The apple glows. The serpent's tongue as well.

The sand along Karl Linne's Alley crunches.
Lazily I am reborn, examine the skies
with amphibian stare.
Is that the place where I will live?
But the family no longer wants me to take them there.

The family tree is rustling malevolently
and all of them are scared.
All of them are bitter.
"Go away!
I don't want to see you, Daddy!"
my future shouts in my face.

He flings the paperbag to the ground.
The ketchup-smothered sandwiches smash

and spread out like the blood of an ancient martyr
whose name has been forgotten.

The branch is broken. Let's not poke about for reasons.
Child, make your own beginning, your own new offshoot,
along which a new eternity can proceed.
And my own end I will invent myself.

But why is no one noticing the split?
People and animals watch each other through the bars.
Meanwhile, I lift the sunset in my hands.
And soon we will vanish without a trace.

I never was as free as now—a beast
having escaped from the political zoo.
So what if across the bridge with its arches of stars
some new century is said to have passed.

I too cross through border forests.
And then I flow into the distant vistas.
Lord, thank you for forgetting
to lock my cage.

2001

# A DOUBLE BALLAD

Here it is—the Twenty-first Century—:
a transparent carafe,
into which nothing has yet been poured.
And our voices resound:
"Man is older than the Earth..."

I know what that would mean, were it true.
Okay.
Add to the account my years, too.
They are
equal to the degrees
of the twice-distilled brandy—
the strong brandy,
which is just about to flow
from the stills to the prophecies
full of lightnings...As for me...
I spring from a wilder distillation.
Flowing doesn't cause the fire to grow weaker.
I don't mix with the delicious weakness of weak brandy.

The Twenty-first Century—
A shout of a prophet having fled from a legend.
A waking of a bird.
Or a howl—
rather an echo of a Bacchante in heat
"Evoe!" she cries.
While I keep hearing: "I'm yours!"
(Forgive me, heavenly lips.)

Yet I keep fancying
that my years will suffice
for two lives
of the one and only God.

I peer through the stellar locks to see
who is pretending to be absent there.

And I see myself walking
through ugly cities
with striking girls.

"Take away my reason and toss it into the sky!"
and I see myself flowing undiluted.
Perhaps a little pungent.
Booze for barbarians,
reaching out for the carafe
of the age, which never came true.
And our voices keep resounding
in your mystic transparence,
Twenty-first Century
of the so-called new epoch,
and second (balladic one) of mine.

2001

# RIDGE

*Those that I fight, I do not hate.*
*Those that I guard, I do not love.*
                    —W.B. Yeats

I would fall asleep on a summit
and wake up on a coast.
Mystery!
And imagine,
this whore is the mother
of the abandoned plays.
But what is taking place there
behind the curtain
of closed eyes?

There the soul is creeping
along the pale and bare ridge
of what has already been.
A picker of herbs for painkillers,
my soul is moving away,
seeking something lost.

I have lost the ability to get drunk.
Not that I have stopped drinking
illusions.
No. They simply
don't go to my head anymore.
And how could that not have happened, since
along the pale and bare ridge
war is striding:
warm, cold,
secret, star and global
or God knows what,

striding as slowly as a sower
and scattering the seeds of deadlock.

Nothing sprouts quicker.
And not that bullets don't ripen for me.
Not at all. Simply,
they don't strike me anymore...
And why
all that feverish rushing?
All those *Poetry Readings, Spells,*
and *Salutes to the Fire?*
Perhaps if I hadn't glanced
so often at my watch,
it wouldn't be so late.

They wouldn't have erected
that castle of sunset
upon the pale and bare ridge.

What do you think,
old buddy, Peter Curman?
Shouldn't we launch the chariots
around the fortress once again?
The beauties meanwhile madly waving
goodbye to us.
Because I have begun to turn into
a pale and bare ridge
that doesn't know
what elemental reins it holds.
Yet it knows that so far
nothing has kept a curb on me.

2001

*Edifice*

# THE WALL

We've agreed with the sunset
that we won't look into each other's eyes
while time keeps flowing
and we are part of that same flight.

The woman artist and I have agreed
that she'll go deaf
and I'll go blind.
Thus
maybe at last,
both of us will be doing the same thing.
As in love axioms,
which are not susceptible of proof
but are taken on trust.

This is why I kiss you, approaching sky.
And you, young new horizons,
pale from perspective.

I, too, used to be annoyed
when my mother would draw me close
and kiss me in front of other people,
feeling that she was losing me.

Youth doesn't value such feelings,
unfailing health,
unconquered truth.
Youth prefers
fables and
love.

And look, in rosy haze
the port of the well-invented Ephes
is empty.

The sailors are in the brothel.
Merchants are trying to outwit
each other in the marketplace.
And politicians are squabbling
after the communal midnight feast.
But the swallows are flying lower and lower,
which portends storm,
broken boughs,
falling nests and universes.
From Ephes to the very Alexandria
a-a-a...an apple.
The apple of discourse.

Old man, what are you babbling about?
How is it that you have eyes?
Why did Basil II forgive you?
Precisely you?
Look, the mountain
carries skies, it is of use.
Why does it have no eyes,
while you still have them?

I try to argue
that the mountain has lakes.

How original!
Would you like us to turn your eyes into lakes
from which bitter brooks will flow?
And ask you then:
What do you see? Ah?

I see.
I see the desert,
global one and promised.
But what are the little children,
the Israeli ones, God's elect, doing there?

We are building up a wall without a temple,
an endless wall is what we're building up,
a new wailing wall.

Eyes, don't say goodbye
to this visible world
and this non-Euclidean space!
For I feel like a manuscript
hidden in the cracks
between the stones of the wall.
Eyes, don't say goodbye!
For I have already been written down
but not yet read.

2005

# THE CAT IS DRINKING
# WATER FROM MY GLASS

For Toma Markov

I know it is a dream.
I know that now
I should move
my hand. Drive it away. And take
a tranquilizer...No,

I can't.

Instead of me,
the reading lamp begins to move.
It takes a different shape,
becomes a starship,
and the little men
get off to take me
as if I were their tranquilizer.

Of course, not the entire me.
My goal,
my axis,
my restless pursuit of an end for itself—
they don't need such things.

They come to wrench from my soul
just one presumptive kernel.
A little ampoule, hidden
behind the wrapping of a glossy consciousness.
But under it...
something mysterious happens.
The little men flee terrified.
But the ship has gone.
I hear a lapping sound...Oh, God!

The cat is drinking from my glass of water.
Thanks, Savior!
Thanks!
Now
my hand will move.
The phantasms will die of fright. And I,
for the lack of a tranquilizer,
will have to gulp down a part of myself...

"You can have some water as well," the cat says.
"For I am only a memory
of your former cat Simmo.
In case you don't believe it,
in case you doubt,
remember Antoine,
remember Lavoisier.
Remember how he was examining water
and instead of a goldfish, he caught
the law, according to which
nothing is created or lost
but only changes its nature...
Then remember the guillotine, where
Lavoisier himself
lost his head.
Adieu, mon cher! Adieu!
Your mother said you shouldn't be afraid.
You won't die in a foreign land.
Beware of water and of fame.
In the present horrid times of form-betrayers,
against the laws—
create!"

2001

# NOT FAR FROM THE SHORE

Not far from the shore
I am standing on credible walls.
A useless plant with aerial roots.
And under me
seven ages
have already been excavated.
Seven doubles of yours
watch me from under broken helmets.
Troy, Troy, Troy,
how mine you are!
Yet, there is no trace to follow to my own self.
Nothing of what has happened has survived,
except the shadow of the blind poet,
who has hardly been here.
Meanwhile, I'm standing on the walls.
And why should I see
the dirt road
and the field,
where rag-countrymen are waving sleeves about?
Whom do they scare?
What do they guard?
Only the bales of straw
shine scattered
like plundered sarcophagi.
A fiery wind blows.
and I hear the interrupted phrases of the scarecrow:
Menelaus chased Paris
for the beauty which
didn't save the world.
Achilles fought the duel with Hector
over the corpse of friendship—
the soul's heel.
And you, Time, windy or quiet,

various and continuous,
whom do you fight?!
Is He that strong?
And what's it all about?!
Yet, whatever it's about,
have done with it!
For I am sick and tired
of scaring birds.
I'm already scared myself!

Dauntless little tractors haul
green mountains of watermelons.
Some tourists ask me
whether I am the archeologist.
They blabber that the war is over.
But isn't that red horse
grazing
in the bed of a river run dry,
a gift brought by the Greeks?

And the heart is open.

2002

# SEMANTIC SEEDS

For Alexander Taylor

Listening to poems in a foreign language—
this indeed seems like
paranormal phenomena,
contacts with nonexistence,
painting a landscape
beyond the mist, ready to tell you:
"Oh, it's not this!
Not this, not this at all!..."

In my neighborhood there is a pipe,
which sings gutter-like
prophecies to the wind.
No clattering of tin. No whistling.
But music.
A melody.
A public prayer.
I have tried to go out in the dead of night to look for it,
to make out the magic.
But it falls silent instantly.
"Don't be afraid!"
I say to it...
I don't care
what follies you spread
but how you do it...

For instance, Lazlo Nod,
whenever God blessed him with good humor
and illimitable alcohol,
used to translate Bulgarian folk songs.
"Dilmano-Dilbero," et cetera,
meant to him:
"A falcon perched on my shoulder."

Since he was lame,
he had to fly
rather than sow.

A horse had kicked him
in his childhood years
and the older ones were afraid to visit.
Thus he became a big child.
Then—a huge child.
Then—an old child.
I don't remember what language we spoke in
so long with Lazi. Then
the winged horse came to take him back.

Look, yesterday Manuel Muños Hidalgo came.
And the table, redeemed forever,
was filled with Castillian exclamations.
Only the glasses gazed with empty looks
when Manolo said:
"I've come to warn you
that the mold they used for us is broken.
They won't be making the likes of us
anymore."

You must talk with things
in their own fragile tongue. Don't fancy
that they understand yours.
If you find a way, show them
that you test them, the way one tastes
desire or boredom,
or the way one tests a student. Then all
the children will start prompting,
signaling, moving their lips.
And if you grasp one single sign,
you already have a significant captive—
a "Tongue," as they used to say on the front lines—

a trace of truth resembling
a mark of wing upon the sky.
Begin right now! But don't forget:
only the lie is verisimilar.

So now, having learnt a lesson from my dog,
I bite my leash myself.
This means that I want to go out.
And to think that I am leading my own self myself.
I want to go out of these wicked words,
robbed by politicians,
slobbered over by poets,
stinking of calumny.
I want to go out of them.
And to love you speechlessly.
And to run across that field.
To leap over the magnetic lines.
To follow the scent of the poles
and to contemplate
the ants dragging semantic seeds.
People don't like the singing insects.
People like the fabulous ants.
And they give me the creeps because
the World is a semantic sign
that cannot be pronounced.

2002

# A TALE
# FROM TWENTY-FOUR THOUSAND,
# FOUR HUNDRED AND FIFTY-ONE NIGHTS

Nevertheless,
some day
I will drink up this damned bottle,
in which
no jinn
has ever been confined
except mine.
But before I leave,
I'll ignite the cork,
just to be sure.
I'll burn it in the ashtray
as if it were a witch.
And with the muddy soot
I'll paint
a black (but not pessimistic)
eye on my forehead
or rather between my forehead and the wall,
which no one could break down.
Yet so many others have collapsed!

"I am the one-eyed one!"
the smoke will utter, rising,
abandoning the fire
(just as my truest little comrades
abandoned me).

I wonder, is there anyone left to say:
"Blinded dreams,
I will lead you
and I will even tell you what can be seen

*Like Grass*

on both sides of the road.
What is seen,
what is seen...is space.
Yet no time
can be seen."

We keep stumbling along the road sought
by the Phoenician King Agenor's
kidnapped daughter.
Which way are his
signs,
signs,
signs
pointing...
But that happened earlier.
And now it's later.

On the celestial display
quietly rise
star wars.

The swindler has gone before us.
And has left
the doors of words open.
The wind is blowing!
It keeps invoking memories.
And the warmth of sentiment grows cold.
And the pipes
along which thought runs
are cracking.
And the glittering ice
strikes roots into dark nothingness.
And is that writing?
Is that speech?
Or are these signs?—
Stolen, crumpled, torn-up, greasy signs

through which the bottom of the bottle
already appears.

This is how the world has gone out of itself.
And in the empty smoky space
the waitress is seated
on the adjacent era.
She has taken off one of her shoes,
wriggling swollen little toes.
And she is writing down
a short story of digits.
"Hey, girl,"
I say,
because I feel like saying something to someone,
"would you tell me a story?"
She gasps:
"Are you nuts, old man?"
which means: Request denied!
"Come on, what's the matter?!
I just want you to narrate my conscience to sleep,
lest I should look at
what's happening around me."
"I know what you're looking at.
But watch out I don't call the barman
to tell you the ending
before you know the beginning."
"If that's what you think,
lie low, Scheherazade's asshole!
I can narrate my sleeping pill
myself."
Once upon a time,
(somewhere between the twentieth
and the twenty-first moments
after the end of history),
there was, you know, one more pitiful ending—
the creature Visionary vanished

from the dying human species.
It became extinct because
it ceased believing
in miracles.
So then dreams went blind.
Because they see
only with visionary's eyes,
having none themselves.
And then
the age of blind luck reigned:
some ate and drank.
while all the rest had little fun.
Finally,
before closing, a madman
suddenly got up and painted that eye on himself...
And people started dreaming again...

The barman dreamily calls the waitress
into the small backroom behind the bar.
She walks past me,
shakes the bottle
and exclaims:
"It's as empty as your head.
Now shake a leg,
because we're gonna sweep away reality."

                    2003

# ULTIMA VERBA

Sometimes it seems to me
that once
everything was a beginning
or in the beginning,
or before that.
And I used to cast myself forward to finish,
                                    to finish.

The way you put out a fire,
lest you go up in flame.
The way you plug up a hole,
lest you sink.
The way you love for the first time
not caring why
or in order to end carelessness.

But, you see, of late,
something draws me to begin,
                        to begin.
And perhaps it's indeed the ultimate time.
I begin a new building on top of the ruins.
I build a wall, and dig, and fill,
until I hear:
"My God!
But you...what are you doing?
You said that you were planting a bush,
yet passion sprouts,
yet fury sprouts!..."
And I watch the crazy plant
with sin-bearing blossoms
and fruit
of the forbidden knowledge.
It is a plant I know.

And I'm ashamed, I'm ashamed
of the present historical tense,
of the shameless tense
with verbs stripped bare.
"I swear to you!
This is impossible!
I planted two little seeds!
I planted Ultima Verba!"
Night passes beneath my window
talking to someone:
"A willow tree?!"
That's a wretched substitute
for the Judaic palm tree, for the olive tree..."
But we feed
not on
only what is spoken,
but only
on what has been understood.

And sometimes it seems to me
that this world is made
of the ultimate words
of other worlds.
Quite other. Quite vanished...
And then I feel
I'm one of them.

2003

# THE STONE

Almost like Sisyphus
and quite like myself,
I heave the stone a little.
Round as a cloud.
Dark as thunder.
Yet what a silence reigns!
Beneath the stone sleeping Evil lies,
a coiled centipede—
a black galaxy with head laid
on a pillow of a martenitsa...
If someone's watching me,
he must be puzzled.
I have to figure out
something comprehensible,
so that the dwarf pats me on the shoulder,
"Good!
You are one of us again..."

I heave the stone
to hide time under it—
the time I stole.
"Why, where can one
steal time?"
Of course I answer you:
From one's self.
Only from one's self.
Most easily, from one's own sleep.
And most laboriously—from one's own work.
"And why steal?...
And from yourself at that...
And time at that!"
To give Love
something purely mine.
"And she? What did she say?"

She told me that she couldn't possibly accept
a gift so dear.
She wouldn't like to feel
obliged... To be bound...
That sort of thing.

I used to fix the price of time
according to the pain of parting.
"Time is money"—
to me that was merely
a proverb,
spread by
proverbial Franklin.
However, when I found out
that everyone thought so,
when I saw
my present—a withered
posy, left
without water,
I made up my mind to bring
time back, where
it had been—in me. Then
the stolen time smiled at me:
"Everything comes back, my boy:
the departed swallow,
the prodigal son,
the stolen horse,
the lost hope...
Everything comes back, my boy,
only time,
only time
never returns!"

And look
the cunning metal device
walks across the desert Mars.

It's seeking water.
I am hardly so thirsty.
But I too
am seeking something.
I'm looking for a proper place.
And I look with one of my eyes
at what that one, the metal one, is doing.
Everything there is stone.
Why doesn't it think
of lifting one up too?
And what will happen
if a martenitsa flares up again
under it.
You wonder what?
I'll tell myself:
This is a proper place
to close my eyes.

2005

# ASHES OF LIGHT

## I

I have found a house,
older than the universe.
And master-builders turned up right away.
Well, you've bought
quite a white elephant there,
they said.
Actually, old age is irremediable.
Better to pull it down
and make
something entirely new
out of the material,
as the last of the leaders used to say.
But you don't seem convinced,
so make your repairs.

I said: "I'll think about it."

## II

All night long my lantern burns.
I can think in the dark just as well.
But I take delight in seeing
how the sunset nestles into me,
and how in the morning
it tiptoes away.
And I pretend that I don't hear.

## III

The room looks like a lantern
and I,
perhaps,

like a wick burning low.
Ashes of light.
Nocturnal creatures bat against
my glass walls.
Enormous moths with crimson eyes
on their wings keep fluttering about.
You are like us, they say to me,
only you have wings on your eyes.

IV

And in the morning, the birds wake me up.
Their little beaks are knocking,
announcing a tranquil destiny.
In fact, they breakfast on the moths
stuck on the window-panes.
Then they tell me:
Beware of the master-builders!
They are keen on making repairs
because there is a legend:
in the foundations of this house
is hidden the treasure
of the dead caravan.

V

What demon has started the rumor
that in the foundations of this world
there is a treasure
of virgin happiness?

I don't mean sphinxes
sacred chalices,
talking tables
and alchemic witchcraft...
Yet, the caravan of time

is loaded with secrets,
isn't it?

VI

Since I am too shy to beg,
I adjure:
Be wary of
the master-builders
who offer
to repair our world.

2005

# DISTANCE XXI

"You're so far away,"
you whisper in my ear.
Instead of kidding around,
you'd better fasten your seatbelt!
I am fastened to those same circumstances.
The stewardess, expressionless as a ghost,
demonstrates how to put on
and inflate a life jacket.
All too frequently now
display replaces hope.
Everything is explained
in two languages.
One of them is as condemned as love.
I think God spoke in fewer words.
Take a look at which are His
and which have been made up
later on
by us.
And choose for the two of us
something unique,
something condemned...
No,
distance isn't
such an almighty cause.
As is the case with flying,
it's more important how many wings you'll change,
at how many airports you'll be waiting
for the fog to lift...
I hate this impenetrable emptiness.
So, first kiss me.
Then I'll confess to you:
We can't fly for long.
We land too often.
We have to check

whether the Earth has fled.
We have to drink the melting snow—
it is Eternity in a state of change...
Now we are rising
over the dark predictions.
Our phones are turned off,
lest we be troubled
by the cries for help,
by the gurgling of cut throats
or by the gunshots within the temple...

It's time for emergency measures!
It's time to take prints
from fate's finger.
The world situation is dualistic.
But when was it not?
The Virgin has given birth to twins.
Apropos,
I saw such a painting
at the cheerful exhibition
"Rubens' Years" or something like that.
The author hadn't had the courage to sign his name.
They had removed the haloes of the infants.
To humiliate them completely,
they had placed them
on welfare...
Only an eagle is entitled to two haloes.
All of us are looking suspiciously at one another.
One of us is a terrorist.
One of us will blow up the flying heart.
Or will be shot before that
by the friendly fire
of liberty.
And this will happen within us,
not somewhere else.

So, darling,
I'm not that far,
I'm not that far,
from the truth.

2005

# IRISH FANTASIES

To Celia and Jack


1.

The ninth wave has cast me up
upon the isle of Achill.
Around me the rocks are smoldering
like bits of cinder
fallen from the northern lights.
Magic streams
flow down from the nothingness
and merge together.
And the waterfalls of Dookinella
bark now and then like dogs
made up by Heinrich Böll.

Of course, I think about
the parting. And "I drink
to keep my body and soul
separate,"
as Oscar Wilde said.

Otherwise,
everything is
simple and lonely.
And the clouds keep quiet.
As if
God is writing His memoirs.

A repentant devil whets lightnings.
And I slowly turn into an island.
According to the bell that is impossible

but in Connemara they sing a song,
according to which
along the road northwestwards
slow things happen.


2.


The strangely humble cottage
of the Nobel laureate,
after his death, was turned into
a home for strangers,
for poor wretches writing memoirs
and drinking "Paddy."

All night long the rain returns
to knock at the windows
like a drunkard.

I conceal the fact that I feel cold.
But
Jack Harte, the ambassador of birds,
goes out and returns with a pail of peat.
The hearth bursts into flames
with the smell of malt.

They say claustrophobia
is a disease of poets.
It catches me
when I think about the German
locked up in himself.
Then I start to feel pressed for room
within myself.
The adjacent fence is made of barbed wire
that in turn is wrapped in thick undergrowth
with crimson blossoms

called Christ's tears...
Yet, in spite of that,
or maybe just because of that,
everything has managed to escape,
everything that
had any meaning.

Now I feel so bookish,
that I am writing on my own self—
unrepentant and
with unsharpened lightnings.

    3.

I return to Dublin
like a bolt out of the blue.
What, damn it, have you been doing up there?!

Dublin's chimneys
are arranged
like mouth organs,
like Latin libraries
or Russian Katyushas.
Or maybe they are combs
for combing nimbus clouds.
But they don't suspect it
and they fancy
that they are mystic crowns.
"Lord!"
they say,
"What a small world,
and what a large number of rulers we got to be!"

And it seems they are right.

If a star falls down,
it serves it right.
If a ruler falls,
what a laughter will follow.
But if a chimney falls!—
It's an omen
for the entire universe,
which is already choked with smoke.
And everyone rushes forward
to lift the chimney up again—
the fire's crown,
the raven's rostrum.

And let God lift His nose
from the blurred screen.
Let Him turn off the computer
and conclude:
There is a time for everything.
A time for memories.
And a time to wear a nightcap.
And a murmur follows:

Goodnight, light.
Bye-bye, God!

2005

*Plovdiv Pan*

# LULLABY

The boy was standing at the exit
of the new gas station
like a deadlock,
like a gas pump,
like an air hose.
I braked suddenly to pick him up.
And only then did I notice
what an evil appearance he had.
I asked him:
"Which way?"
"To Plovdiv," the hitch-hiker grumbled.
"Eh!" I joked bluntly like an intellectual.
"Such a young boy
to such an old city!"
"Oh, fuck this face of mine!
Could you, too, guess
that I still have no ID card?"
"But why are you cursing?"
"Because they won't give me a job.
I can't get started.
Do you know what it's like
to be
and yet be unable to make a start?..."
I gave him a piece of chocolate.
He ate it up at once
and fell asleep.
I watched him, just in case,
in the rearview mirror,
rocking
in the loop of sleep.
His hair, long as a wig,
made him look like
a premature Robespierre.

And so we flew across eternity
like two centuries,
like two tenses:
past continuous
and a future that cannot begin.
Meanwhile the whirling wind hummed a lullaby:
Sleep, sleep, my boy.
It's not your face that's to blame,
but our shameless falseness.
Sleep, but don't trust Fukuyama.
History exists.
History is searching.
And soon
it will find you a job.
Oh, what a job!
They will remember you!

2005

# SMS

To Iva

Did you see the sign of the sunset?
A field sown with secrets.
Rays sprout among the clouds.
Late birds
gracefully alight
and peck early-risen stars.
I only know that these are not landscapes.
Everything is silent and impossible.
Ask the sky what it wants to say.
You can.

2005

# INSOMNIA

Quite close by,
behind the corner of the world,
shines the nonstop
Internet Café.
What was there earlier?
Well, I don't remember.
We gave technology for that.
Electronic databanks of the universal knowledge.

Sometimes my dog
takes me out for a walk
after midnight.
The air is dirty.
The trees are drugged.
Life—imaginary.
His snout touching the blue shopwindow,
my best friend watches
the café's
mystic interior.
At this hour
it is empty and interstellar.
The computers look like
urns for dead time.
Just one display is glimmering.
The hacker is sitting in front of it.
He is creating a virus.
He is sipping cold coffee and dreams
of deleting the memory of the Universe.
What will the world soul
do then?
Where will it hide?
What will it pretend to be?
"It serves it right," the hacker says.
And the dog is bewildered.

He starts shivering
like a clairvoyant in a trance.
Perhaps he sees how the virus
is devouring the past
and over chaos hovers
just a lonely, endless
and uncertain global future.

2005

# NIGHT KNIFE

*Ibidem.*
There is no change.
No stars. The only street
lights are a few shopwindows
and a sign.
Further down is the disco.
Taxicabs—yellow dogs—squatting
in front of the butcher's
for tender flesh.
But nowadays no one abstracts such concepts.
Whereas here it's different. Here
there is a living soul.
It belongs to the guard, who keeps an eye
on the chairs and tables
in front of the new pub.
He has leaned his back on the blackboard
with the unwiped menu.
He has wrapped himself up
like a sensitive, shivering scarecrow.
Nothing can be seen of the soul,
but it sees everything.
The scarecrow sees how
the infinitive tense appears,
how the shade of time sways.
And halts
abruptly...
"That's the thief!"
the guard whispers.
"That's the criminal element.
But what's it doing there? Did it fall asleep?
If so
day will never break!"
And the night guard moves in Time's direction,
armed with just a night knife—

a pocket one, but sufficient.
On his soul's back—
a chalky price.
Whereas everything else is priceless.
And while we ask ourselves:
"Is that life?"
time is suddenly gone,
leaving only
a yellow puddle.
And on the wall, among the meaningless graffiti,
a few more scribbles:
God forgives.
TIME—doesn't!

2005

# SPIDERMAN

In the garden,
in front of the windmill,
not on the bench
but on the grass,
the Spiderman is sitting.
He's opened his paper,
pretending to read the spider's web,
while actually listening to
the desperately buzzing
captured news.
But no one pays any attention
to that postmodern piece of plastic art,
except the sparrows, who are curious
if the flies are real
or fake.
Of course, they are fake—
ready to become history.

Oh, sparrows! Oh, shaggy guttersnipes,
oh, who don't even make nests.
Otherwise, I would have assumed
that it was you, who made us.
Because,
man abandoned by history
is like an abandoned nest.

The inhabited nest
knows it's worthwhile.
Songs come floating out of it.
And that's worthy of praise.

The abandoned nest broods ghosts.

There is a time for making nests,
the Preacher will say.
Then God provides
his special mud.
Nature provides the straw.
We—labor.
And here comes history
and lays its cuckoo's eggs
in us.
Some kick them out of the nest at once.
Others listen carefully:
What is it moving about in there?
"Gosh, it's my heart,"
the others say.
And a new minor history
with a cannibal's little beak
hatches from the heart.

Man, possessed of history,
wants to fly away from himself.
He flaps the wings
he doesn't have.
He is great, if he perishes.
He is wretched, if he survives.
For it's not him but history that flies off.
Then he climbs down
his thin
posthistoric thread
into the nothingness.
Into ordinary time,
which has neither cause
nor consequence.
There, in the garden
of the windmill
(which is grinding unity
into powder)

the Spiderman,
thin-legged
and big-bellied,
is knitting his newspaper, thinking:
If a strong wind blows,
it will bring down the old nests.
That's fine.
But it will also turn over this page.
And something new may happen.

2005

# FALL

Mornings I wander upwards to the forest waterfalls—
tiny children's toys lost by the gods.
Older than the forest, younger than the heavens,
I still feel like playing. I can still be taken by surprise,

being various, yet the same, whereas they are always different.
I called one "My" so it wouldn't be without a name.
It is sunny there. I strip down to my waist.
But I visit it in the winter too...

So even in the bitter cold, I set forth again. And through the mist,
there on the cliff, I saw, instead of the waterfall, a fallen angel,
a quiet, icy body with stooping wings
and a fox licking its tears before running away.

The boreas had toppled down two spruces
as if it wished to carry the wounded creature
on a stretcher from a Simberg painting.
Meanwhile I keep on asking myself absurd questions:

Why do white angels visit us more and more seldom?
Why is the soul's luminous ecstasy breaking apart?

Why does every faith begin in love and end in cruelty
with broken wings of victories, angels, and ideals?
But the next day there was just a tiny cloud sailing way up high.
The waterfall boomed—a white wind had blown past from
                                        Drama or Kavala.

                                                      2005

# Notes

**Moonless Calendar**
Mouncho: the village madman in Ivan Vazov's novel *Under the Yoke*, who, as
the author notes in the final line, was the only person who dared to protest
the Turkish massacre, for which they hanged him.

**Path**
The Mafia throws a lamb's head in front of the door of the condemned
person.

**Ridge**
Mysteries: antic bacchanalian revels, from which theater orginated.
Peter Curman: contemporary Swedish poet.

**The Wall**
Basil II Bulgaroktonos [Bulgar slayer] (957-1025): Byzantine emperor (976-
1025) captured a Bulgarian army numbering 15,000 and ordered that they
be blinded, leaving one eye to each 100$^{th}$ man, to lead them to the palace of
the Bulgarian Tzar Samuil.

**Semantic Seeds**
Lazlo Nagi (1925-1978): Hungarian poet.
"Dilmano Dilbero" ("Pretty Dilmano"): a Bulgarian folksong about a
woman sowing peppers.
Manuel Hidalgo: contemporary Spanish poet.

**The Stone**
Martenitza: a token related to an old Thracian custom preserved in Bulgaria
until the present. On the first day of March, marking the coming of spring,
people give one another tokens of red and white threads for good health and
good luck. After the coming of the first migrating bird, the token is tied onto
a blooming tree or is hidden under a stone.

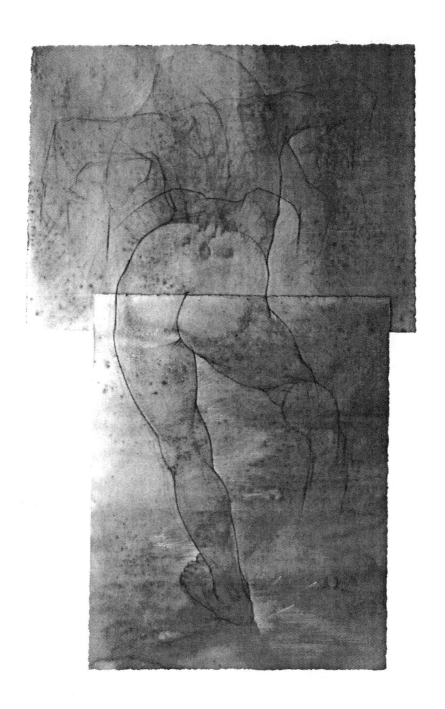

*There Must Be Sacrifices*

LYUBOMIR LEVCHEV was born in Troyan, Bulgaria, in 1935. A graduate of the University of Sofia, he has served the literary community in a number of capacities, including as Chairman of the Union of Bulgarian Writers, First Deputy Minister of the Bulgarian Ministry of Culture, and Editor of the international magazine *Orpheus*. He is a member of the European Academy of Science, Art, and Culture and the European Academy of Poetry.

He has published over 20 volumes of poetry and won numerous awards for his work, including the prestigious Gold Medal for Poetry from the French government and the Mate Zalka and Boris Polevoy awards in Russia. His poetry has been translated into numerous languages, including Czech, English, French, German, Greek, Hindi, Italian, Polish, Russian, and Spanish.

A leading figure from the "April generation" of poets who came into prominence after de-Stalinization in 1950, Lyubomir Levchev has achieved both critical and popular acclaim, and is widely recognized as the pre-eminent living poet in Bulgaria today.

MARK GERARD MCKEE was born in Pittsburgh, Pennsylvania, in 1956. He is a graduate of the Lyme Academy of Fine Arts and has studied at the School of Visual Arts in New York. In 2002 he was the first American artist awarded a Bulgaria Artist Residency as part of the Bulgarian-American Exchange program, sponsored by The Griffis Arts Center and The Orpheus Foundation. From 2002-2004 he held an Urban Artists Initiative Residency, funded by the National Endowment for the Arts and the Connecticut Commission on the Arts in partnership with the Institute for Community Research. His work is in direct response to a personal exploration of the complexities that define our perceptions of reality, the inner struggles for identity, the pathos and banality of everyday life and its visual experience.

Poet and translator VALENTIN KRUSTEV was born in Bulgaria in 1949. His poetry collection, *Between Heaven and Earth*, was published by Orpheus Press in 2005. He has translated extensively from English and Russian, including books by Joseph Brodsky and William Meredith. His translations from and into English have appeared in numerous anthologies and literary magazines.

JACK HARTE, founder of the Irish Writers' Union and the Irish Writers' Centre, has visited Bulgaria frequently. The author of a number of collections of stories, his fiction has also appeared in literary journals and anthologies in Ireland, Britain, United States, Australia, New Zealand, Finland, Bulgaria, and Russia. His translation of a selection of Levchev's poetry, *And Here I Am*, was published by Daedulus Press in Ireland in 2003.

# CURBSTONE PRESS, INC.

is a non-profit publishing house dedicated to literature that reflects a
commitment to social change, with an emphasis on contemporary writing
from Latino, Latin American and Vietnamese cultures. Curbstone presents
writers who give voice to the unheard in a language that goes beyond
denunciation to celebrate, honor and teach. Curbstone builds bridges
between its writers and the public – from inner-city to rural areas, colleges to
community centers, children to adults. Curbstone seeks out the highest
aesthetic expression of the dedication to human rights and intercultural
understanding: poetry, testimonies, novels, stories,
and children's books.

This mission requires more than just producing books. It requires ensuring
that as many people as possible learn about these books and read them. To
achieve this, a large portion of Curbstone's schedule is dedicated to
arranging tours and programs for its authors, working with public school
and university teachers to enrich curricula, reaching out to underserved
audiences by donating books and conducting readings and community
programs, and promoting discussion in the media. It is only through these
combined efforts that literature can truly make a difference.

Curbstone Press, like all non-profit presses, depends on the support of
individuals, foundations, and government agencies to bring you, the reader,
works of literary merit and social significance which might not find a place
in profit-driven publishing channels, and to bring the authors and their
books into communities across the country. Our sincere thanks to the many
individuals, foundations, and government agencies who have recently
supported this endeavor, including: Community Foundation of Northeast
Connecticut, Connecticut Commission on Culture & Tourism, Connecticut
Humanities Council, Greater Hartford Arts Council, The Griffis Foundation,
Hartford Courant Foundation, Lannan Foundation, National Endowment
for the Arts, and the United Way of the Capital Area.

Please help to support Curbstone's efforts to present the diverse voices and
views that make our culture richer. Tax-deductible donations can be made
by check or credit card to:
Curbstone Press, 321 Jackson Street, Willimantic, CT 06226
phone: (860) 423-5110   fax: (860) 423-9242
www.curbstone.org